Remember
the 5th of
November

First published in 2007 by
Franklin Watts
338 Euston Road
London
NW1 3BH

Franklin Watts Australia
Level 17/207 Kent Street
Sydney
NSW 2000

A CIP catalogue record for this book is available
from the British Library.

ISBN 978 0 7496 7414 4

Series Editor: Melanie Palmer
Series Advisor: Dr Barrie Wade
Series Designer: Peter Scoulding

Printed in China

Franklin Watts is a division of
Hachette Children's Books,
an Hachette UK company.
www.hachette.co.uk

HOPSCOTCH HISTORIES

Remember
the 5th of
November

By Mick Gowar and Mike Phillips

FRANKLIN WATTS
LONDON•SYDNEY

About this book

Some of the characters in this book are made up,
but the subject is based on real events in history.
In 1605, a group of men plotted to kill the Protestant
King of England, James I, and blow up Parliament.
They wanted England to return to the Catholic religion.
On 4th November 1605, guards found a man in the
cellars under Parliament, hiding 36 barrels of gunpowder.
The man said his name was John Johnson but he later
confessed to being Guy Fawkes. Soon afterwards, the
rest of the plotters were caught and joined Guy in the
Tower of London. They were all tried and executed.

Once, I was a hero. I helped save the King and Parliament from being blown up. Here is my story ...

I was one of Lord Monteagle's servants. One night, I went to the inn to get some wine for my master's supper.

Some men were inside, whispering:

"Guy – you guard the gunpowder.

On the 5th, you light the fuse and – "

They stopped when they saw me.

I bought the wine and left.

One of the men from the inn

followed me outside.

"Take this letter to Lord Monteagle,
and hurry!" he said. Then he
disappeared into the dark.

I ran back as fast as I could and gave my master the letter.

Master looked shocked. He stopped
eating and got up.

13

"We must show this letter to Lord Salisbury at once," said my master.

We rode to Lord Salisbury's house as fast as we could.

Lord Salisbury read the letter. "There's a plot to cause trouble at the opening of Parliament," he said.

"The King is in danger! Take these men. Search Parliament and all the houses nearby."

Master and I rode through the dark
streets of London to Parliament
with the King's guards.

"Some men have rented that house. Its cellars go right underneath Parliament," a woman told us.

"Search the cellars!" said the Captain of the guards. My master and I followed them inside.

A man was in the cellars.
"Who are you? What are you
doing?" asked the Captain.

"I'm John Johnson," said the man.
"I'm just getting firewood ready
for the winter."

"He's lying!" I said. "I've seen
that man before. He was at the
inn the night I was given the
letter. His name is Guy."

"Search behind those logs!" ordered the Captain. We found 36 barrels of gunpowder. It was enough to blow up everyone in Parliament!

"Seize him!" ordered the Captain.

"Take him to the King!"

Guy was taken to the King's bed
chamber. The King was woken up.
"This man plotted to kill you!"
said the Captain.

"Take him to the Tower!"
commanded the King. "We will
know everything, and those to
blame will be punished."

So when you light bonfires and sing your song: **Remember, remember the 5th of November, Gunpowder, treason and plot ...**

Remember me too, and how I
helped to save the King's life.

For more titles go to:
www.franklinwatts.co.uk
or
www.itsfuntoread.co.uk

* hardback